Storms

By Mary Draper

Contents

Introduction

Storms happen all around the world. There are many different types of storms.

A storm can bring wind and rain. There is often thunder and lightning.

Sometimes the wind picks up sand or dust and blows it very hard.

When it is snowing, a strong wind can blow the snow around and make a snowstorm.

Powerful storms can destroy everything in their path.

Some storms are over in less than an hour. Others can last for several days.

The Weather

The weather is always changing. One day it is warm and dry. The next day it could be cold, windy, and wet. The weather changes when the temperature in the air changes.

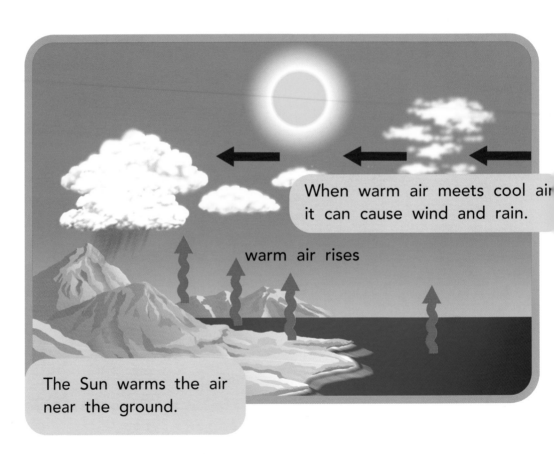

When warm air meets cool air it can cause wind and rain.

warm air rises

The Sun warms the air near the ground.

Storms happen when cold air and hot air mix and make the air spin.

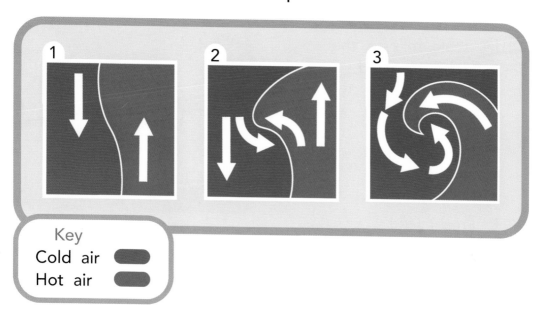

Key
Cold air
Hot air

Then the winds become fierce, and the clouds become heavy with water.

The Beaufort Scale

This scale tells us the speed of the wind.

1. Light air
2. Light wind
3. Gentle wind
4. Moderate wind
5. Fresh wind
6. Strong wind
7. Moderate gale
8. Gale
9. Strong gale
10. Storm
11. Violent storm
12. Hurricane

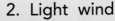

2. Light wind

8. Gale

DID YOU KNOW?

Over two hundred years ago, Francis Beaufort invented a way to measure wind speed.

4. Moderate wind

6. Strong wind

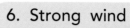

10. Storm

12. Hurricane

Thunderstorms

Thunderstorms bring rain, lightning, thunder, and sometimes hail.

Inside a thundercloud, the warm and cool air mixes and spins. High up in the cloud, drops of water turn into ice. These tiny drops of ice get shaken about. The shaking movement makes an electrical charge.

This charge can become lightning. Thunder is the sound made by lightning. They happen at the same time, but we see the lightning before we hear the thunder.

DID YOU KNOW?

If thunder is heard
as soon as lightning flashes,
the storm is very close.

Hurricanes

A hurricane is a very strong storm that starts over warm parts of the ocean. It usually lasts for many hours. Another name for a hurricane is a cyclone.

The middle of a hurricane is called the eye, and it is quite calm. When it arrives, people sometimes think that the hurricane is over, but it is only halfway through.

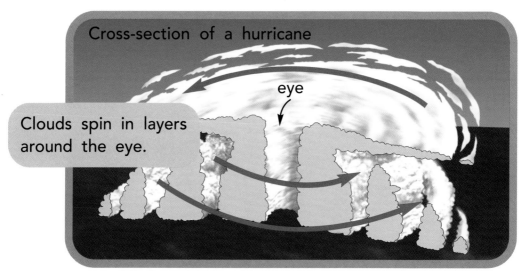

Cross-section of a hurricane

eye

Clouds spin in layers around the eye.

A hurricane spins and moves forward at the same time. As the winds travel across the sea, they make big waves, and water is sucked up into the eye of the storm. The water and waves can cause floods when the hurricane reaches the land.

Tornadoes

Tornadoes happen on the land. They have very strong winds and destroy most things in their path. Tornadoes are smaller and faster than hurricanes. It is easy to see a tornado as it moves across the land.

A tornado spins very fast and makes a funnel. When the funnel touches the ground, it works like a giant vacuum cleaner and sucks things into the air.

Tornadoes usually last for less than an hour, but they cause terrible damage. They can flatten whole cities, and people can be injured, or even killed.

Sometimes things like cars and animals get sucked up into the funnel, and dropped down again a long way away.

DID YOU KNOW?

The United States has hundreds of tornadoes every year.

Dust Storms and Sandstorms

Dust storms happen in places where the soil is dry and there are not many plants to hold the soil together. Strong winds pick up the soil and blow it away. Dust storms can last for days.

DID YOU KNOW?

A funnel of dust that spins around is often called a dust devil.

Sandstorms happen in deserts. Large amounts of sand are picked up and carried along by strong winds.

People and animals must find shelter during a sandstorm. Sand can block the nose and eyes, making it very hard to breathe or see.

Snowstorms

Snowstorms happen when snow has been falling for some time, and the wind gets strong. The wind blows the snow along, and makes it difficult for people to see far ahead.

If the wind gets very strong, and snow continues to fall, the storm becomes a blizzard.

People who are caught in blizzards often lose their way. They can die from the cold.

Predicting Storms

Scientists use many different machines to find out when a storm is going to happen. Some machines measure the speed of the wind.

There are weather satellites in space. They send back pictures and information about the weather on Earth.

Weather balloons are sent up into the sky. They send back information about winds and clouds.

Special ships in the ocean are used to gather information about storms.

Computers help the scientists to understand all the information.

Scientists can usually warn people that a dangerous storm is coming. This may save many lives.

Keeping Safe

People need to stay safe during storms. In some countries, there are special shelters that are very strong and can hold a lot of people. People can even sleep in the shelters if they need to.

Sometimes a room is built under the ground. A family can find shelter there during a tornado.

During a dust storm or a sandstorm, people try to find shelter in their houses, behind rocks, or in tents.

During a blizzard or a thunderstorm, people stay inside.

We cannot stop storms from happening, but we can learn to live with them.

Questions

1. What did Francis Beaufort invent?
2. What does it mean if thunder is heard as soon as lightning flashes?
3. How do scientists name hurricanes?
4. Which country has hundreds of tornadoes every year?
5. What is a dust devil?
6. How far ahead can scientists predict the weather?

Glossary

charge   a store of electrical energy

damage   ruin or wreckage

funnel   something that is shaped like a cone, with a wide top and a narrow base

gale   a very strong wind

moderate   of medium strength

satellite   a large machine with computers that is sent into space and circles Earth

temperature   how hot or cold something is